Ohio Politics

Paul A. Sracic
Youngstown State University

William C. Binning
Youngstown State University

Los Angeles | London | New Delhi
Singapore | Washington DC

FOR INFORMATION:

CQ Press

An Imprint of SAGE Publications, Inc.

2455 Teller Road

Thousand Oaks, California 91320

E-mail: order@sagepub.com

SAGE Publications Ltd.

1 Oliver's Yard

55 City Road

London, EC1Y 1SP

United Kingdom

SAGE Publications India Pvt. Ltd.

B 1/I 1 Mohan Cooperative Industrial Area

Mathura Road, New Delhi 110 044

India

SAGE Publications Asia-Pacific Pte. Ltd.

3 Church Street

#10-04 Samsung Hub

Singapore 049483

Printed in the United States of America

ISBN 978-1-5443-3035-8

This book is printed on acid-free paper.

Acquisitions Editor: Monica Eckman

Editorial Assistant: Sarah Christensen

Production Editor: Tracy Buyan

Typesetter: Hurix Digital

Proofreader: Annette Van Deusen

Cover Designer: Michael Dubowe

Marketing Manager: Erica DeLuca

18 19 20 21 22 10 9 8 7 6 5 4 3 2 1

Contents

The Role of Ohio in National Politics

In the eighty-two-year span between 1841 and 1923, the United States elected twenty-one different individuals as president. Eight of those presidents, or nearly forty percent, were from Ohio. Only the state of Virginia has given the nation more presidents. Since Ohio native President Warren G. Harding's death on August 2, 1923, however, no Ohioan has sat behind the desk in the Oval Office. Nevertheless, Ohio remains at the center of U.S. presidential politics. During the final weeks of the 2016 campaign, for example, the two major party campaigns spent more than $12 million on campaign ads in Ohio. Only Florida enjoyed more financial attention from the campaigns.[1]

Will Ohio remain important in presidential politics? That might depend on population growth within the state. With every new census, Ohio's representation in Congress, and therefore the total number of electors representing the state, declines. In 1964, Lyndon Johnson gained twenty-six votes by capturing Ohio. When Donald Trump won Ohio in 2016, however, only eighteen electoral votes were earned. In a sense, therefore—and again, by looking at the numbers—Ohio is becoming less and less significant in presidential politics. So why is Ohio still considered, even by the candidates themselves, a crucial "battleground state" in U.S. presidential elections? There are two related reasons.

When political pundits talk about "red states" and "blue states," they are acknowledging that, even before anyone casts their vote in a presidential election, it is not hard to predict with a high degree of certainty which party's candidate will ultimately win the popular vote. Republicans dominate in "red" states, and Democrats control "blue" states. So, for example, the two most populous states (and therefore the two most electorally rich states), Texas and California, are not currently considered competitive.[2] It is a foregone conclusion that Texas is "red" and will support the Republican candidate, while a majority of voters in "blue" California will cast their ballots for the Democratic Party's nominee. Texas and California are not alone when it comes to states that are considered noncompetitive. A total of thirty-eight states and the District of Columbia are considered fairly solid red or blue states. That leaves twelve so-called swing states. In swing states—Colorado, Florida, Iowa, Michigan, Minnesota, Nevada, New Hampshire, North Carolina, Ohio, Pennsylvania, Virginia, and Wisconsin—the outcome is difficult to predict, because voters "swing" back and forth from election to election, between the Republican and Democratic candidates. Of these states, only Florida and Pennsylvania have more electoral votes than Ohio.

Swing states are also sometimes called "purple states," since their electoral status is derived from the near equal numbers of solid red and blue voters. Using this definition, it is hard to imagine a state more purple than Ohio. For example, if one adds up all the Democratic votes for president between 2000 and 2016, and then compares that number to all the corresponding Republican votes during that same period, the difference is only about 290,000 votes out of more than 266 million cast. This comes out to a difference of about one percent. (See Table 1.) Beyond electoral votes and the closeness of presidential races in Ohio, there is an additional argument to be made about the significance of Ohio in presidential campaigns. As Figure 1 shows, Ohio, demographically, is somewhat of a microcosm of the United States. In other words, with the notable exception of the very low number of Hispanic voters in the state, Ohio "looks" like the United States. From this perspective, Ohio is important because it is an ideal test market for political candidates.

If a candidate is popular in Ohio, they are likely to have qualities that will appeal to voters throughout the United States. Hence winning Ohio is important not because of the electoral votes gained, but because of what it says about a candidate.

Purple State Politics

More than fifty years ago, Thomas A. Flinn, a political science professor at Oberlin College, wrote a much-cited article describing Ohio politics.[3] Reading that article today, it is remarkable how much of what

Table 1 Presidential Vote Difference, 2000–2012

Year	Democrats	Republicans
2000	2,186,190	2,351,209
2004	2,741,167	2,859,768
2008	2,940,044	2,677,820
2012	2,827,709	2,661,437
2016	2,394,164	2,841,005
Total	13,089,274	13,381,239

Source: Author created from data from https://www.sos.state.oh.us/elections/election-results-and-data/#gref.
Note: Total Votes cast = 26,470,513.
Difference = 291,965.
% Difference = 1%.

Flinn documented in 1960 remains unchanged. Flinn concluded, for example, that, "Ohio is now and has long been a competitive two-party state in which Republicans have an advantage."[4] He based this statement on the partisan results in presidential, gubernatorial, and state legislative elections in Ohio from 1895 through the 1958 election. Using these same data points for the years beginning in 1960, one finds similar results. From 1895 until 1958, Flinn found that Republicans won ten presidential elections, while Democrats came out ahead in six contests. From 1960 through 2016, the numbers are almost exactly the same, with Ohio voters giving at least a plurality of their support to Republicans in nine of the fifteen contests. Gubernatorial elections, however, tell a slightly different story. By a count of nineteen to twelve, Flinn's study found that Democrats had been more successful than Republicans. Beginning in 1962, however, with the election of Republican James Rhodes, the GOP reversed the trend, and winning ten out of fourteen gubernatorial elections held through 2014. These increasing gains for Republicans are also reflected in the state legislature. Flinn found that, in the Ohio Senate, Republicans held a majority twenty-one times, while eight Senate elections were favorable to Democrats. The Senate was tied twice (something that could not happen after 1967, when the size of the Senate was set at thirty-three, an odd number). The Republican trend in the Senate became even more exaggerated after 1960. Indeed, Democrats have not controlled the Senate since 1984. Where Flinn had found the House "somewhat more Republican than the Senate," recent results do not bear this out. The Democrats controlled the Ohio House of Representatives for most of the 1980s, and although losing

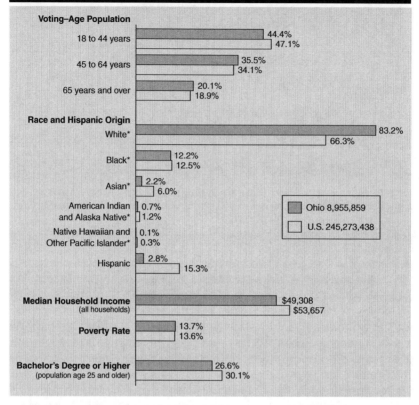

Figure 1 Ohio Demographics

Voting–Age Population

18 to 44 years — 44.4% / 47.1%

45 to 64 years — 35.5% / 34.1%

65 years and over — 20.1% / 18.9%

Race and Hispanic Origin

White* — 83.2% / 66.3%

Black* — 12.2% / 12.5%

Asian* — 2.2% / 6.0%

American Indian and Alaska Native* — 0.7% / 1.2%

Native Hawaiian and Other Pacific Islander* — 0.1% / 0.3%

Hispanic — 2.8% / 15.3%

Ohio 8,955,859
U.S. 245,273,438

Median Household Income (all households) — $49,308 / $53,657

Poverty Rate — 13.7% / 13.6%

Bachelor's Degree or Higher (population age 25 and older) — 26.6% / 30.1%

Source: Data from the U.S. Census Bureau, https://www.census.gov/content/dam/Census/library/visualizations/2016/comm/cb16-tps44_graphic_voting_ohio.jpg.
Notes: In combination means in combination with one or more other races. The sum of the five race groups adds to more than the total population because individuals may report more than on race.
* Alone or in combination, non-Hispanic.

their majority after the 1994 elections, returned to power for two years following the 2008 elections (see Figure 2).

The end result is that Ohio is a state that leans Republican in state races, but tends to give its votes almost equally to Republicans and Democrats in presidential contests. It is this latter fact that gives Ohio its "Purple State" identity. Even this statement, however, must be qualified. For when one looks at the election results tallied by each of the state's eighty-eight county boards of elections, one does not find many "purple" results. Instead, one finds counties that are consistently deeply red (Republican) and others that are just as blue (Democratic).

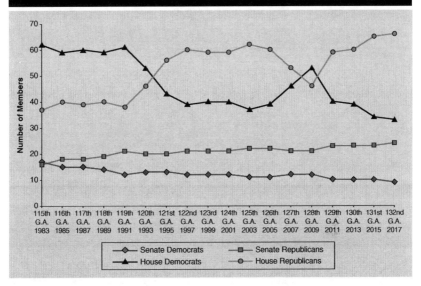

Figure 2 Political Party Affiliation and Transfer of Majority Membership in the Ohio General Assembly (1983–2017)

Source: Data from the Ohio Legislative Service Commission, *A Guidebook for Ohio Legislators*, https://www.lsc.ohio.gov/documents/reference/current/guidebook/appendixe.pdf.

The "Five Ohios, and the Rural-Urban Divide"

Over the years, analysts have come up with various templates to try to both categorize and to explain these different voting patterns found throughout the state.

Perhaps the most popular way of understanding the diverse politics of Ohio is to divide Ohio up into five regions. This "Five Ohios" approach identifies the distinct political orientations of Northeast, Northwest, Southeast, Southwest, and Central Ohio. Northeast Ohio is the most Democratic region in the state. Historically, the Democrats' strength in this corner of state is countered by strong Republican voting in the opposite corner of the state, in Southwest Ohio. The Northwest, Central, and Southeast regions of the state have tended to be more competitive. In addition, however, economic history and past migration patterns also seem to influence present day voting. For example, the strong Republican leanings of the Southwestern part of Ohio has been linked to the fact that early settlers to the area were anti-slavery Southerners from Virginia and elsewhere whose descendants gravitated to the Republican Party.[5] At the same time, the fact that Northeast Ohio was once the home to large, unionized, manufacturing facilities helps to explain the strong and (until 2016) consistent Democratic vote found in these counties.

As one looks at the results of the most recent presidential races in Ohio, however, the "Five Ohios" approach seems to be breaking down. Hamilton County, the largest county in Southwest Ohio, supported the Democratic candidate for president from 2008 through 2016. At the same time, Southeast Ohio has become solidly Republican, at least in presidential contests. In 2012 and 2016 all of the counties in Southeast Ohio except one (Athens County, home of Ohio University) supported the Republican nominee for president.

It is becoming increasingly evident that the rural-urban division is now the best way to explain the partisan vote in Ohio. Parts of Ohio that are more densely populated gravitate toward Democrats, while less populated areas tend to support Republicans. Between 2008 and 2016, the Democratic nominee for president won at least seven of the ten largest counties in Ohio. At the same time, Republicans received overwhelming support in most smaller counties, sweeping nine of the ten smallest counties in 2008, and ten of ten in 2012 and 2016.

Ohio: A Brief History

Although Ohio's identity as a "battleground state" is based on its assumed status as a must-win state for both major political parties in presidential contests, the term might also be understood in a more literal sense: The area that would eventually comprise the state of Ohio was the proximate cause of a real war that indirectly contributed to the establishment of the United States as an independent nation.

Michael Barone and Richard Cohen have suggested that Ohio might rightfully be called the "first entirely American state," since it was the first state with no direct connection to one of the former British colonies.[6] Ohio was never a separate colony under British rule, but was part of a disputed area known as the Northwest Territory. This territory, bounded roughly by Pennsylvania, the Ohio and Mississippi rivers, and the Great Lakes, was prized by the European powers, particularly Britain and France. In 1749, King George II granted a charter to a Virginia group known as the Ohio Company for lands south of the Ohio River.[7] Although this area was technically not part of the Northwest Territory, it did involve lands claimed by France. The eventual response by France culminated in 1755 with the French and Indian or "Seven Years" War. The Treaty of Paris, which in early 1763 formally ended the conflict, gave the British title to the Northwest Territory. Possession passed to the newly freed colonies at the conclusion of the American Revolution.

Northwest Ordinance

It the aftermath of the Revolutionary War, it was difficult to determine which, if any, of the thirteen newly independent states actually controlled

Figure 3 Northwest Territory (1787)

Source: David B. Scott, *A School History of the United States, From the Discovery of America to the Year 1878*. New York: Harper & Brothers, 1879, p. 222. Courtesy of the private collection of Roy Winkelman. https://etc.usf.edu/maps/pages/3900/3904/3904.htm.

the Northwest Territory. The original British charters establishing the colonies extended their dominion to undefined and as yet unclaimed territories to the west. Arguably, Virginia, New York, and Connecticut could all claim portions of the Northwest Territory and the land that would become Ohio.

The ratification of the Articles of Confederation, the first U.S. Constitution, was initially delayed by the question of whether the various states would forgo their claims over the Northwest Territory to the new central government.[8] This matter was eventually resolved, and the Articles of Confederation Congress took control of the lands. The Congress passed laws in 1784 and 1785 attempting to apportion out the territory and establish a path to statehood. Finally, in July of 1787, as a new U.S. Constitution was being drafted in Philadelphia, the Articles of Confederation Congress approved "An Ordinance for the Government of the Territory of the United

States Northwest of the River Ohio." This became known as the Northwest Ordinance.

The Northwest Ordinance called for the territory to be divided into "not less than three nor more than five States," with the three initial states called the Western, Middle, and Eastern. The Eastern state was to lie between the Ohio river and the Canadian border, bounded on the east by Pennsylvania, and on the west by a line "drawn due north from the mouth of the Great Miami [river]."[9]

From a Territory to a State

Five officials, all appointed by Congress, initially governed the Northwest Territory. In addition to a governor, there were three judges and a secretary. Acting together, the governor and the three judges formed a four-member legislature. The Northwest Ordinance mandated the establishment of an elected legislature once the population of free males in a territory exceeded five thousand.[10] By 1798, the governor of the territory, Arthur St. Clair, determined that the population was sufficiently large, and voters were asked to choose members to their first elected territorial legislature.[11] When the new legislature convened in 1799 in Cincinnati (it would move to Chillicothe in 1800), it consisted of an elected House of Representatives and a five-member appointed Legislative Council. One of the first tasks for the new legislature was to select a nonvoting delegate to represent the territory in the U.S. Congress. Given Ohio's later role in selecting presidents, it is perhaps fitting that they chose a future president, William Henry Harrison. Of course, Harrison was not a full-fledged member of Congress, because Ohio was not yet a state. In fact, one of the major issues to be addressed by the General Assembly involved whether the territory should petition Congress for statehood.

Even at this early stage in our nation's history, the area that was to become Ohio was directly tied to national political struggles. The two major political parties at the time, the Federalists and the Republicans, were divided on the question of statehood for Ohio. Both parties suspected Ohio would be a Republican state, and if it became a state it would increase the power of the Republicans in Congress. As a result, the Federalists, led by Governor St. Clair, wanted Ohio to remain a territory.

In 1800, congressional Republicans took the first step toward statehood for Ohio by passing a law dividing the Northwest Territory into two sections, with the eastern division encompassing the area that would become Ohio. By the spring of 1802, the Congress passed a resolution authorizing the inhabitants of the eastern division of the Northwest Territory to form a state government, allowing that once such a government was formed it would be "admitted to the Union upon the same footing as the original states." In response, the General Assembly convened a convention to draft a state constitution. Elections were held in October, and on November 1, 1802, the thirty-five delegates who were elected met in the town of Chillicothe. Twenty-nine days later, they had hammered out a document calling for an Ohio government consisting of a governor, a two-house legislature, and a judicial branch.[12] On February 19, 1803, the U.S. Congress passed another act in which it acknowledged both the state's constitution and the formation of Ohio's government.

The manner in which the Congress chose to admit Ohio led to an ongoing debate about when precisely the Territory became a state. The year 1803 is commonly used, based on the February 19 acknowledgment by the Congress. Arguably, however, Ohio became a state in November of 1802, when the state constitution was ratified, thus "forming" a government for Ohio. This became more than just a point of contention among historians. Since the actual date of admission could not be specified, one could make the argument that Ohio was not really a state! Because of this, in 1953 a congressman from Ohio, George Bender, proposed a bill retroactively admitting Ohio to the Union as of March 1, 1803. The bill passed both houses of Congress and was signed by President Eisenhower in the summer of that year.[13]

The Ohio Constitution

1802 Constitution

The basic outline and wording of the first Ohio Constitution followed closely the outline of the U.S. Constitution that had been drafted only fifteen years earlier. Even the placing of the listing of rights at the end of the document resembled the Federal Constitution, which had seen the Bill of Rights added as a set of amendments a few years after the ratification.

There was, however, one critical sense in which the 1802 Ohio Constitution differed from the 1787 U.S. Constitution. The U.S. Constitution established a fairly strong executive, while the governorship in Ohio would be much weaker. This may have been a reflection of the fact that the 1802 Convention was dominated by Republicans, a party which, consistent with the ideas (though not necessarily the later presidential actions) of its leader, Thomas Jefferson, believed strongly in rule by the many, and therefore preferred multimember legislatures to single member executive. Under the 1802 Ohio Constitution, the governor was to be directly elected to a two-year term but, unlike the members of the legislature, was term limited and could not serve more than six years in an eight-year period. More significant was that the Ohio governor was not granted the power to veto legislation. This meant that the General Assembly had the final word on laws of the new state of Ohio.

The 1802 Constitution provided for a two-house General Assembly. Members of the lower house, the Ohio House of Representatives, were to be directly elected and were to serve a one-year term. The number of representatives was not determined in the constitution, but the number was to be proportional to the population, and at least until the white male population over the age of 21 exceeded 22,000, could not exceed thirty-six representatives. The reference to the "white" male population merits some mention. The convention at first voted to include African Americans among voters. A motion to strike this provision passed by the narrowest margin possible, with the president of the convention, Edward Tiffin, breaking a 17–17 tie.[14]

The House was to share legislative authority with a Senate. As was the case with the House, the number of senators was not specified. The only requirement was that the number of senators could not be less than a third, nor more than half the total number of members in the Ohio House of Representatives. The senators would serve a two-year term, which would be staggered so that one-half of the senate would stand for election every year.

In addition to passing laws to govern Ohio, the General Assembly was to have additional tasks not shared with the governor, including electing the secretary of state, state treasurer, and state auditor. In addition, the two houses of the legislature were to elect the three judges who would form the Ohio Supreme Court, as well as the several judges who would serve on the three courts of common pleas in Ohio.

As already noted, the final article of the 1802 Constitution contains a rather extensive listing of rights. Along with protections for freedom of religion and speech, and an affirmance of the right to trial by jury, the 1802 document also contained an absolute ban on both slavery and poll taxes. The 1802 Constitution concludes with a reminder to the state that "all powers not delegated, remain with the people."

Section 5 of the penultimate article of the 1802 Constitution, Article VII, states that, any time after 1806,

> whenever two-thirds of the General Assembly shall think it necessary to amend or change this constitution, they shall recommend to the electors, at the next election for members to the General Assembly, to vote for or against a convention, and if it shall appear that a majority of the citizens of the State . . . have voted for a convention, the General Assembly shall, at their next session, call a convention. . . .

It would take Ohioans nearly half a century to avail themselves of this mechanism.

1851 Constitution

Ohio grew rapidly in the early days of the 19th century, and this caused a particular problem for the state supreme court. Article III of the

1803 Constitution called for the supreme court to hold sessions "once a year in each county." As the number of counties increased, this began to place great burden on the four judges who served on the state's highest court. When one of those judges, Ethan Allen Brown, became governor in 1818, he encouraged the legislature to place the question of whether to convene a new constitutional convention before the voters. The legislature acquiesced, but the measure was soundly defeated in 1819 by a vote of 29,315 to 6,987.[15] By the late 1840s, however, with Ohio having expanded to eighty-two counties, the situation for the supreme court became unbearable. After much political wrangling, the legislature voted on March 23, 1849, to place another call for a constitutional convention before the voters of Ohio. This time, the measure passed by a vote of 145,698 to 51,161.[16]

The convention began its work in Cincinnati on the first Monday in May of 1850. Once again reflecting the national politics of the day, the convention was closely divided politically, with newspapers reporting that about fifty-four percent of the delegates were Democrats, with the rest being Whigs and a handful of Free Soilers.[17] The convention worked until early July, and then reconvened on the first Monday in December before adjourning on March 10, 1851. The constitution that they produced was ratified by the voters in the state of Ohio on June 17 of that year, and went into effect about two and a half months later, on September 1.

The 1851 Constitution consisted of sixteen articles (now expanded to eighteen). Unlike the 1803 Constitution, the 1851 document begins with a Bill of Rights that closely tracks the first ten amendments to the U.S. Constitution. Beyond the addition of a listing of rights, the 1851 document differed in several other ways from its 1802 predecessor. First, the court system was restructured, with the onerous requirement that the supreme court meet annually in each county replaced by the provision that newly formed district courts—consisting of common pleas court judges and one judge from the supreme court—fulfill this mission. The supreme court was expanded to include five judges, and all state judges were to be elected.

In a like manner, the 1851 Constitution took the election of the governor, along with the secretary of state, auditor, and treasurer out of the hands of the Ohio legislature. All of these offices, along with the newly created positions of lieutenant governor and attorney general, would form an executive branch and be directly elected by the people of Ohio. All but the auditor, who was to serve for four years, would be elected biannually. The lieutenant governor would function much like the U.S. vice president, serving as the president of the Ohio Senate while only being allowed to cast a vote in the case of a tie.

Article 16 of the 1851 Constitution contained provisions to amend the constitution. There were two basic methods. First, if three-fifths of both houses of the General Assembly voted in favor of any proposed amendment, it would be placed on the ballot. Alternatively, two-thirds of both houses of the General Assembly could vote to call a convention, which could then "revise, amend, or change" the constitution. Regardless of how these amendments were proposed, they would become part of the constitution if they received support from a majority of voters who participated in the election. This meant that a proposed amendment could receive a majority among those who voted on the amendment, yet not be approved because that majority was less than a majority of all those who actually showed up to vote on the day of the election. Finally, beginning in 1871 and every twenty years thereafter, the state was required to place a question on the statewide ballot asking: "Shall there be a Convention to revise, alter, or amend the Constitution?" If a majority of the voters said yes, a convention would have to be called. Any amendments proposed by a convention, however, would still be subject to approval by a majority of voters.

1912 Convention

As required in the Constitution of 1851, the question of whether to call a new convention was placed before Ohio voters in 1871. The measure passed, and a convention convened in May of 1873. When the convention finished its work the following May, they had drafted a new constitution, as well as several amendments that were tied to the approval of that new constitution. Foreshadowing changes that would eventually be made to the 1851 Constitution, the convention's constitution expanded both the number of judges on the supreme court and the term for which they would serve. The governor's office was also strengthened with the addition of a conditional veto.[18] The new constitution was submitted to the voters, and was soundly defeated by a coalition that included those who opposed the expanded term for the supreme court judges as well as members of the temperance movement who opposed the amendment on the ballot at the same time that would have allowed for the licensing of alcoholic beverages.[19]

Despite the failure of the 1873 Convention, the voters of Ohio did approve eleven amendments to the constitution between 1851 and 1912. Most significantly, an amendment was approved in 1903 that granted the veto power to the governor.

When the required question of whether to call a new constitutional convention was put before Ohio voters in November of 1910, it passed by the extraordinary margin of 693,203 to 67,718. The convention had such strong support because so many different groups—advocating causes from tax reform to women's suffrage to those on both sides of the Prohibition debate—agreed that a convention was needed.[20]

Delegates to the convention were elected a year later, and the convention began its work in Columbus, Ohio, on January 12, 1912. By the end of May in 1912, the convention had agreed to submit 41 proposed amendments to the 1851 Constitution to the voters. On September 3, 1912, at a special election, thirty-three of these amendments were approved. These amendments significantly altered the 1851 Constitution by, for example, expanding the membership of the Ohio Supreme Court and adding a chief justice, as well as by altering the governor's power to veto legislation. Most significantly, the people of the state of Ohio would now be able to directly initiate both laws and constitutional amendments, as well as challenge by referendum laws already passed by the General Assembly.

Post-1912

As required by the constitution, the question of whether to call a new constitutional convention has been placed before Ohio voters every twenty years. Since 1912, however, it has failed every time, most recently in 2012. Nevertheless, the Ohio Constitution has changed in significant ways over the past 100 years. During that period, Ohio voters have approved more than 120 amendments to the constitution, including adding term limits for all state office holders, defining marriage as between a man and woman, and, in 2010, authorizing casino gambling in the state of Ohio. Despite all of the changes, and the expansion of the Ohio Constitution from its original sixteen articles to its present eighteen articles, the 1851 document has never been completely replaced. House Bill 188, passed by the 129th General Assembly and signed into law in the summer of 2011 by Governor Kasich established the Ohio Constitutional Modernization Commission. This thirty-two-member commission was charged with "making recommendations from time to time to the general assembly for the amendment of the Constitution." In part because of partisan bickering, the Commission was dissolved four years early, in July of 2017. It made some minor recommendations, some of which may find their way to the ballot in the near future.[21]

The Ohio General Assembly

The Ohio General Assembly first convened in Chillicothe, Ohio where it remained until 1813. After a brief two-year stay in Zanesville, the legislature moved to its current home in Columbus in 1816. Under the current Ohio Constitution, adopted in 1851, the legislature is required to meet once every two years. The General Assembly convenes on the first Monday in January in odd numbered years. It meets for a two-year period or biennium, that is divided into two annual regular sessions.

There are ninety-nine members of the Ohio House of Representatives and thirty-three members of the Ohio Senate. An Ohio state senate district is made up of the boundaries' three house districts. Representatives serve two-year terms. Senators serve four-year terms and approximately half are elected every two years. Vacancies in either body are filled by the caucus of the party of the departed member. An appointed House member serves the remainder of the term. In the Senate, if the member who vacated the seat served less than twenty months, then the appointee must stand for election in the next general election and win to serve the remainder of the term. One benefit of an appointment is that the time served as an appointee counts for seniority but not toward the time of the term limit. In the 131st (2015–2016) General Assembly there were eight appointments in the House and one in the Senate.

Membership in the Ohio General Assembly is part-time for some and full-time for others. A member's salary ($60,584) can be enhanced with a leadership role. The Speaker of the House and the president of the Senate make $94,437. The type of occupation a member has, and the distance from Columbus are factors in determining if the member can maintain another occupation. Many Ohio legislators are lawyers and oftentimes continue their practice while they serve in the legislature. A member who lives hours from Columbus will usually arrive in Columbus on Tuesday and leave on Thursday when the legislature is in session. A house member has one staff aide while a senator has two aides. These aides maintain the legislative offices, respond to interested parties, and answer the phones.

There is some diversity in the current Ohio state legislature. Thirty-one of the 132 members in the 132nd General Assembly are women, with a higher percentage serving in the House than in the Senate. There are sixteen African Americans in the 132nd Ohio General Assembly.

Organization

Both chambers of the Ohio General Assembly are organized by a political party. The party with the majority of the seats controls leadership positions and determines the number of committees and committee size. The majority party determines rules and the passage of bills.

The presiding officers in the Ohio legislature are the House Speaker (Cliff Rosenberger, 2014–2018) and Senate president (Larry Obhof, 2017–). The Speaker of the House and the president of the senate wield great influence in the legislature; that power, however, will be lost if the majority is lost. There is also a speaker pro tempore and president pro tempore who are second in command and take charge when the leader is absent and often wield significant influence.

Term limits impact reoccurring leadership selection. The 132nd General Assembly was the last term for Speaker Rosenberger, and that prompted an informal contest for the Speaker of the 134th General

Assembly. Finance Committee Chair Ryan Smith was pitted against former Speaker of the House Larry Householder, who, after being term limited out of his seat, returned to the house in 2016. These leadership struggles take place well over a year from the general election, and the members who participate assume they will be reelected and that their party will retain the majority,

As the head of their respective chambers, the Speaker of the House and president of the senate are charged with preserving the order and decorum in their respective bodies as well as with deciding questions of order and procedure. Some of the formal powers of the presiding officers include:

- Recognizing members who wish to speak during floor debates
- Interpreting and applying the rules of the chamber during floor action
- Appointing members to committees; this includes the power to replace committee members (For example, in 2011, to ensure committee passage of the controversial bill that limited the collective bargaining rights of Ohio public employees, some Republican senators were replaced on the Insurance, Commerce and Labor Committee by the Republican leadership.)
- Acting as chairperson of the all-important Rules and Reference Committee.

The most important job for the Speaker of the House and the president of the senate is to guide bills through their chambers in the legislature. These presiding officers must sign all bills and resolutions enacted by the General Assembly to certify that procedural requirements have been met. One reason the leadership has this responsibility is to make sure that resolutions and bills produced by the house and senate are consistent with the policies of the leaders' political parties. Currently, the Republicans who control both houses of the Ohio legislature make their major policy decisions in their caucuses. These caucus meetings are not open to the public.

An important part of the functioning of the Ohio General Assembly is the committee system. Hundreds of bills are introduced each year by legislators, and committees allow for a division of labor in dealing with what otherwise would be an overwhelming amount of work. At the beginning of each legislative session, members of the majority and minority parties are queried as to what committee assignments they prefer. Former Ohio governor Richard Celeste (D) recalled that, although he was on the wrong side of Vern Riffe's ultimately successful bid to be reelected as Speaker, Riffe still greeted him with the message, "Welcome to the

AP Photo/Chris Kasson

| **Vern Riffe**

Democratic caucus, and let me know what committees you want to be on. We'll do our best to be fair."[22]

Although the Speaker and the president make the committee assignments in their houses, they generally accept the recommendations of the minority leader for minority party membership. By custom, the leadership acknowledges proportionality. Proportionality means that the minority receives their proportion of seats on committees based on the percentage of seats that they hold in the legislative body. Current house rules specifically require that committee membership reflect the proportionality of partisanship in the house. The presiding officers name the chairs of the committees, and these chairs are always members of the majority party.

Both houses make an effort to work out committee schedules so that they do not overlap and interfere with members' attendance. The committee chairperson exercises a great deal of authority over the operation of the committee. The chair can determine when the committee meets, which bills referred to committee will be given a public hearing, the duration of the testimony, and when amendments may be offered. All committees may subpoena witnesses to appear before them for the purpose of testifying on legislation. They can also subpoena *duces tecum* (an order to produce books, papers, records, and other evidence).

The rules of the two chambers require that in order to recommend a measure for passage or to postpone further consideration of bills or resolutions indefinitely, the votes of a majority of all the members of the committee must be obtained; a majority of those present is not sufficient.

There are three main type of committees in the Ohio General Assembly: standing committees, conference committees, and interim committees. Standing committees, at least in the house, also have subcommittees. Subcommittees are made up of a small number of members of a standing committee and are formed to work on some particular aspect of the overall jurisdiction of the committee.

Standing Committees

Standing committees are the main committees through which potential legislation must pass. Standing committees should schedule hearings, propose amendments, and determine the final form of bills and resolutions. Standing committees, through their action or inaction, may also determine which bills and resolutions will be killed and which will be sent to the floor for debate.

Standing committees are formed at the beginning of each biennial session. It is up to the leadership to determine the number of standing committees, although many of the most important standing committees are simply re-formed in every session. The number of standing committees in the Senate in the 132nd General Assembly is thirteen and the Finance Committee has four subcommittees under the Finance Committee. In the house there are twenty-one standing committees with six subcommittees under Finance.[23]

Rules and Reference Committee

Although the Rules and Reference Committee is technically a standing committee, this committee has quite different functions from other standing committees. The Rules and Reference Committee, of each assembly, plays a role at both the beginning and the end consideration of legislation. In addition to referring bills and resolutions to other committees, the Rules and Reference Committee schedules floor votes by the full house and senate once bills and resolutions leave committees.

Conference Committees

If legislation does not pass both houses in the same form and one house cannot be convinced to simply accept the other house's form of the bill, then a conference committee is formed with members from both houses. They are charged with resolving the differences between the two bodies. At the end of a legislative session, conference committees become very important. In fact, much lawmaking goes on in these committees as amendments are added and language is changed. At times, bills produced by a conference committee can bear little resemblance to the original bills that were supposed to be reconciled. The most notable conference committee is the one usually formed at the end of the biennial budget cycle.

The Law-Making Process

A bill is a result of an idea that comes from a legislator, a constituent, a state agency, or an interest group. It is put in the form of a bill by the nonpartisan Legislative Service Commission. It is then offered by a General Assembly member for the purpose of having it enacted into law. The process is complex, with bills going through committees, and having to be passed by both the house and senate prior to final approval. If a bill passes in both the house and the senate it then becomes an act. If an act is approved by the governor, or if the governor fails to veto a bill within ten days, then it becomes a law. In the end, very few bills are actually passed into law. In the 131st General Assembly, for example, only 182 of the 1,004 bills introduced became law.

The most significant and time-consuming legislation is the biennium budget bill. Ohio is one of the few governments that adopts a two-year operating budget. A specific appropriation made by law is required for the state to spend money. Work on the budget occurs primarily in the first six months of the biennial session of the General Assembly. Invariably the budget deliberation process goes on until the very last day of the fiscal year and a conference committee is needed to resolve differences between the two houses.

The Ohio Constitution requires that each bill receive consideration on at least three different days by each house before it is enacted. A member files a bill with the House or Senate Clerk and it is then numbered by the House or Senate clerk. It is first considered when the title is read and then it is referred to the House or Senate Rules and Reference Committee. The second consideration occurs when it is referred to a standing committee.

A standing committee holds public hearings on proposed bills; this is an opportunity for proponent and opponent testimony. It is also an opportunity for lobbyists to testify and show its client that the lobbyist is working for the preferred outcome. The committee may amend or create a substitute bill and may postpone, defeat, or favorably report the bill. The bill may be discharged for further consideration. The bill then goes to the Rules and Reference Committee, which may schedule a bill for third consideration (floor action).[24]

When the Rules and Reference Committee schedules a bill for floor debate and a vote, it is placed on Calendar; at that point it receives its third consideration. It can be amended, placed on the table, defeated, or approved. If it is approved, it is sent to the second house for the same process. If the second house passes a version of the bill other than the first house version and they do not concur either house can call for a conference committee. A conference committee usually consists of three members from each house appointed by the Speaker of the House and president of the Senate. If the differences are resolved, a conference committee report is submitted to both houses for approval, no changes can be offered. If it is approved, it becomes an act for the governor's approval.

The governor does not have a "pocket veto" like the president of the United States; if the governor does nothing the act becomes a law after ten days. The governor may veto any act of the General Assembly. Also, the governor of Ohio may veto items (line item veto); in any act containing appropriations. After a veto, the act is returned to the originating house and three-fifths of the members may override the veto; it then goes to the second house for the same required vote to override. The act becomes law despite the governor's rejection. The Ohio Constitution requires ninety full days for a law to go into effect to permit any possible referendum petition.

Controlling Board

The current form of the Ohio State Controlling Board was created in 1969. It is presided over by an appointee of the Office of Budget and Management and has six legislative members, two of whom by statute are chairs of the House and Senate Finance Committees. The remaining members are appointees of the legislative leadership (with two from each house), including one member from each of the major political parties. The Ohio State Controlling Board is a unique institution in that has both executive and legislative powers.[25]

The Ohio State Controlling Board has extensive power under Ohio law. The board can do the following:

- Transfer funds within an agency or move appropriated money for one agency into another agency's budget.

- Authorize the expenditure of capital appropriations for purposes other than originally provided for in the capital appropriations act. When doing this, however, the board cannot authorize the use for these funds for operation purposes.

- Alter the requirements for advertisement of bids for construction, repair, or other improvements of any building, and

- Waive competitive bidding requirements for specified types of contracts, the Controlling Board has authority over leases that exceed a certain amount.

Perhaps the most significant regular authority of this unique board is that no monies can be released for capital construction without the approval of the Controlling Board. The most controversial decision by the Controlling Board was its response to Governor John Kasich to have the Ohio State Controlling Board bypass the General Assembly and expand Medicaid under the Affordable Care Act. The expansion was opposed by Republican majorities in the General Assembly in 2013, so Governor Kasich asked the Controlling Board to make the decision to adopt the federal offer to expand Medicaid and approve spending $2.56 billion and expand Medicaid insurance to 275,000 Ohioans. The vote by the Controlling Board was 5 to 2. Randy Cole, the chair of the Controlling Board and the governor's representative, voted yes, as did the two Democratic members. At the last hour, the Speaker of the House and the president of the Senate replaced members on the Controlling Board to provide some Republican legislators' votes for the expansion.

The following day, the Ohio-based 1851 Center for Constitutional Law filed a suit with the Ohio Supreme Court on behalf of six members of the Ohio House of Representatives. The suit contended the Controlling

Board exceeded its authority when it voted to expand Medicaid. The Ohio Supreme Court agreed to an expedited hearing on this matter, and in December of 2013, by a vote of 4 to 3, agreed to uphold the action of the Controlling Board and stated that the Controlling Board had the authority to accept and spend the federal Medicaid funds.

Reapportionment and Redistricting

Every ten years a census is taken and then the congressional seats are reapportioned to represent the changes in the population of the states. The drawing of district lines for both federal and state legislative seats is controversial. The party controlling the process is often accused of "gerrymandering." Gerrymandering means to draw districts to achieve a particular political result. Usually, the result desired is to secure as many legislative seats as possible for the party controlling the process.

As has already been discussed regarding Ohio's importance in presidential years, Ohio has lost seats in Congress over the years. Congressional districts are drawn by the Ohio General Assembly, and with the benefit of an elected Republican government controlling the process, the new districts yielded twelve Republicans and four Democrats.

A slightly different process is in place for drawing state legislative districts. There are currently thirty-three state senate districts and ninety-nine state house districts (see Figure 4). The boundaries of the state senate districts are derived by combining three Ohio house districts. In the early 1960s, Ohio's state legislative districts, like those of many states, did not meet the standard of one person one vote established by the U.S. Supreme Court in *Reynolds v. Simms* (1964). After considerable controversy, the Ohio Constitution was amended in 1967, and a five-member Apportionment Board was created to draw the state legislative district boundaries. That board consisted of the governor, the auditor, and the secretary of state as well as one person chosen jointly by the Speaker of the house and the leader of the senate from the same political party as the Speaker. The fifth member of the board had to be a person of the major political party of which the Speaker in not a member. This ensured that at least one member was from each of the two major political parties. The Ohio Republican Party rebounded in the 2010 election, and took control of the three administrative offices on the Apportionment Board. This allowed them to control the redistricting process for the drawing of the new district boundaries for the 2012 election.

On November 3, 2015, a legislatively referred constitutional amendment creating a new bipartisan commission was approved by a statewide yes vote of 2,226,822 to 849,043 no votes. The proposal was supported by the Ohio Republican Party, League of Women Voters of Ohio, Common

Figure 4 Ohio State House Districts

Ohio House Districts 2012-2022
(As Adopted 2012)

Source: The Office of the Ohio Secretary of State, https://www.sos.state.oh.us/globalassets/publications/maps/adopted-house.pdf.

Cause of Ohio, and the Ohio Democratic Party, as well as numerous other organizations. The amendment, which takes effect in 2021, creates a seven-member board called the "Bipartisan Ohio Redistricting Commission." The members of the commission are the governor, state auditor, secretary of state, one person appointed by the speaker of the House of Representatives, one person appointed by the legislative leader of the largest political party in the House of which the speaker is not a member, one person appointed by the president of the Ohio Senate and one person appointed by the largest political party in the Senate of which the president is not a member. To approve a plan for ten years, at least two members from each major political party have to agree to the plan. If this new commission fails to pass a plan by a bipartisan vote, the members are to pass a plan with a simple majority of four members; this plan, however, will only last four years (not the usual ten years). Political and governmental leaders are not certain how this new system will work since it will not be tested until after the 2020 census.

This new system will not impact drawing the new congressional district after the 2020 census. That will still be done by the Ohio General Assembly unless one of the initiative efforts to change that process is passed.

Direct Democracy in Ohio

In 2017, the Ohio General Assembly continued to deliberate on a bipartisan proposal to curb gerrymandering for Ohio's congressional districts. A group called Fair Districts=Fair Elections was skeptical of the legislature, and was continuing to pursue collecting signatures for an initiative which, if passed, would turn power over congressional redistricting over to the Bipartisan Redistricting Commission that will after 2020 be used for state legislative districts.[26]

The early 20th century progressive movement was influential in Ohio. A good example of this was when, in 1912, Ohio adopted a constitutional amendment providing for an initiative and referendum.

The initiative allows citizens to initiate both constitutional amendments and state laws by signing petitions and then voting on the proposals. The procedures and requirements for amending the Ohio Constitution by initiative (a direct initiative) are slightly different from those required to add a state law (an indirect initiative).

There are two independent sets of signature requirements when citizens seek to amend their constitution through the initiative process. First, before signatures can be gathered in support of placing an initiated amendment on the ballot, the Ohio attorney general is required to certify that the language summarizing the proposed amendment in fair and truthful. A petition signed by at least one-thousand Ohio voters must accompany the submission to the attorney general, along with the names of three to five individuals who will represent the petitioners. After certifying the summary, the attorney general sends it and the text of the actual amendment to the Ohio Ballot Board. This is a five-member board consisting of the secretary of state and two members from each of the two major political parties.

Once the summary and text of the proposed amendment has been certified, many more signatures must be gathered for the proposal to be placed on the ballot. In order for a proposed amendment to be placed before the voters, signatures equal to ten percent of the total number of voters who cast ballots in the most recent gubernatorial election must be collected and placed before the secretary of state. There is also a distributional requirement that signatures equal to five percent of the gubernatorial vote must be obtained in half (forty-four) of Ohio's eighty-eight counties. If the requirements are met the proposed constitutional amendment is placed on the ballot in the next general election, and must be approved by a majority of those voting on the issue.

The procedure for a constitutional amendment is considered a direct initiative, and does not have to be submitted to the General Assembly for approval before it is placed on the ballot. Ohio is only one of eighteen states that allow its citizens to propose constitutional amendments by using the initiative.

The 1912 constitutional amendment that gave the citizens of Ohio the right to use the initiative for constitutional amendments also permitted the citizens of Ohio the opportunity to use the initiative to place proposed state law before the voters. The process begins with one thousand signatures being gathered and approval gained from the attorney general and the ballot board. Then the supporters must collect three percent of the voters in the last gubernatorial campaign in support of the proposed statute, including 1.5 percent of the votes cast in at least forty-four counties. If the signatures are determined to be sufficient by the secretary of state, then the proposed law goes before the General Assembly. If the General Assembly amends or fails to act within four months, then the proponents have the option of collecting the same percentage and distribution of signatures as had been required to place it before the General Assembly, and it is then placed on the general election ballot. If there is a majority in favor, it then becomes law. It is not subject to a gubernatorial veto. This type of initiative, which is required to first go to the General Assembly is called an indirect initiative.

Another part of Ohio's direct democracy that was adopted as a result of the constitutional convention of 1912 was the referendum. This word has a distinct meaning in Ohio's Constitution. It gives the people the power to challenge laws recently enacted by the General Assembly. It is similar to a gubernatorial veto. The petition challenge, which requires three percent of the vote case in the last gubernatorial election, has to be filed within ninety days after the governor files a law with the secretary of state. The law is then suspended pending the outcome of the challenge by referendum. Those challenging the law then must collect the signatures of six percent of the vote that was cast in the last gubernatorial election. If the challengers succeed, the question of the law goes on the general election ballot. For the law to be upheld it needs a majority of yes votes. While this constitutional right of the people in Ohio is used infrequently political observers believe a "no" vote is easier to achieve than a "yes" vote in a referendum test.

The most notable recent referendum focused on Senate Bill 5, placed on the ballot though the use of the referendum procedure. Senate Bill 5, passed by the Republican controlled General Assembly and signed by

Governor John Kasich, limited the collective bargaining rights of public employees. The challenge mounted by Ohio's unions defeated this anti-union law in 2012.

An anti-union "right to work" initiative was placed on the ballot in 1958 and soundly defeated. An initiative limiting marriage to a male and a female was passed in Ohio in November 2004. It was viewed by some observers as a scheme to increase turnout for the Republican ticket. That limit on same-sex marriage was nullified by the 2015 U.S. Supreme Court decision in *Obergefell v. Hodges*. Hodges was Ohio's health director, under Governor John Kasich. Legalized gambling was a reoccurring initiative in Ohio. After five attempts, gaming interests finally succeeded in 2009. That initiative was financed by national gaming interest with significant state interests. It created monopolies in four major cities: Cleveland, Columbus, Cincinnati, and Toledo. The initiative also created the tax on the casinos, the recipients of that tax, and a regulating authority, the Casino Control Commission. In November 1992 a term limit initiative was successful in Ohio. It included limits on federal officials, which were later deemed unconstitutional by the U.S. Supreme Court, as well as on state officials, which remain in place.

An initiative to legalize recreational and medical use of marijuana was placed on the ballot for the Fall 2015 election in Ohio. It was soundly defeated, sixty-five percent to thirty-five percent. Polling showed much greater support for recreational use of marijuana and overwhelming support for medical use of marijuana. It is likely that this particular issue failed because the interests that financed having it placed on the ballot proposed in the measure a monopoly of producers. The ten sites were already determined as part of the proposal. The Ohio General Assembly did move to legalize medical marijuana in Ohio. That law was implemented in 2017.

The use of the initiative by self-interested groups, such as the gaming and marijuana growing industries, has led to calls to raise the vote for passage of initiatives to a super majority. Ironically, if that proposal were to ever reach the state ballot, it would be required to be passed by only a simple majority vote.

The Executive Branch in Ohio

The Ohio Constitution stipulates, "The supreme executive power of the state shall be vested in the governor." Since 1978, a lieutenant governor has been elected in tandem with the governor. Prior to that they were elected separately. There are four other constitutional executive offices that have defined administrative functions that are separately elected. This executive fragmentation, however, does not diminish the fact that the Ohio governor is considered a strong governor on measures of formal institutional power.[27]

The term of the Ohio governor is four years, with a two-consecutive-term limit. The Ohio governor has vast appointment powers, a major role in budget making, clemency authority, and a strong veto power that can only be overridden by a three-fifths vote of the legislature.

The effectiveness and strength of the Ohio governor does not rest solely on the constitutional authority of the office. The role of governor is central to Ohio government and politics, and makes the governor the chief policy promoter and advocate in Ohio.

Prior to 1959, the governor of Ohio was elected to a two-year term every even numbered year. Ohio voters adopted an amendment in 1954 expanding the term to four years with a two-consecutive-term limit. The amendment went into effect in 1959.

Ohio Governors

Ohio gubernatorial candidates are not political novices. Most of them are seasoned Ohio state politicians who, with very few exceptions, began their careers in the Ohio General Assembly.[28] Election to a lower statewide administrative office has been a common route to the governor's office. On occasion, candidates have gained their party's nomination directly from a local office, usually after being elected a mayor of a large Ohio city. Some of the most notable Ohio political figures of the later part of the 20th century served as big city mayors before becoming governor of Ohio. Frank Lausche (D) served as mayor of Cleveland, Michael DiSalle (D) served as mayor of Toledo, and James A. Rhodes (R) served as mayor of Columbus before becoming state auditor and then the longest serving governor in Ohio history. George V. Voinovoich (R) served in multiple Cuyahoga County offices, then as lieutenant governor, followed by mayor of Cleveland before he was elected governor of Ohio.

The last two governors, Ted Strickland and John Kasich, served in the U.S. Congress as their last elective office before being elected governor. Neither had run statewide before being elected governor. These two thus defied the old Ohio political adage "one to meet, twice to win." David Sturrock and his coauthors wrote that "every Ohio governor and U.S. Senator elected since 1958 has previously lost at least one statewide race."[29]

The Roles of the Ohio Governor

The various roles played by Ohio's governor are quite similar to the role played by most governors throughout the nation. These include functioning as the head of state, legislative leader, chief budget official, chief of state security and safety, grantor of clemency for state offenses, party leader, crisis manager, and finally intergovernmental coordinator.

The Office of Ohio Governor John R. Kasich

Congressional Pictorial Directory, 109th

| John Kasich | Ted Strickland

As head of state, the governor of Ohio is the top dignitary in the state. As governor, he or she is to appear at official ceremonies and public events. Ohio governors especially enjoy cutting ribbons for new and expanded businesses in the state, particularly if they can take credit for it. Governor Bob Taft christened many of the new and remodeled school buildings constructed as part of the state's response to school funding decisions made by the Ohio Supreme Court. The Ohio governor also speaks for Ohio on the national stage and is expected to be on the scene in cases of natural and man-made disasters and crises, even if the state can do little about it.

The governor has a significant role in setting the legislative agenda for the Ohio General Assembly. The governor will lay out his agenda at the annual State of the State address. The governor biennial budget is usually the working document for the legislature.

Relative to other states, the budget-making power of the governor of Ohio is "very strong."[30] Every two years, the governor submits his biennial budget four weeks after the new General Assembly begins (there is an extension to March 15 for newly elected governors). The executive budget becomes the budget document to which the legislature responds. As it is in nearly every state, Ohio is not allowed to run a formal budget deficit.

Formal and Informal Powers

The Ohio governor has extensive veto power, including a *line item veto*. Kasich line item vetoed forty-seven items in the 2017–2018 budget. The major items were restrictions on the Medicaid expansion, which he vetoed. The legislature overturned the veto on six items, the most significant was the language restricting the governor's legislative power in the use of the Controlling Board. The conservative Republicans were still irritated by

Kasich's Medicaid expansion. The legislature did not override Kasich's veto of the limits placed on the Medicaid expansion.

An informal legislative power of the governor is access to the state media to promote his or her legislative agenda. The governor is able to travel around the state and talk to Ohio's fragmented media market about the legislative proposals. Although Governor Kasich enjoyed a unified government throughout his tenure, he had limited success with his legislative initiatives. One of the problems might have been that Governor Kasich appeared to announce his policy proposals before talking to the legislative leaders.

The Ohio governor has the power to call out the Ohio National Guard to respond to emergencies. There are occasional natural disasters such as floods and snowstorms in Ohio. There can also be manmade threats to life and property. In one of the most tragic events in modern Ohio history, Governor James Rhodes called out the Ohio National Guard to maintain order during the student antiwar protests at Kent State in 1970. That ended with the death of four people. In January 1978, Governor Rhodes called out the Ohio National Guard to plow snow and rescue stranded motorists in what was the worst snowstorm to hit Ohio in sixty-eight years. Rhodes was very visible in the state's response to that crisis and that is credited with helping him get re-elected to an unprecedented fourth term in November of that year.

In the 1980s Governor Dick Celeste, a Democrat, tried to stop the Ohio National Guard from being deployed in Honduras for training exercises. The governor lost that battle in federal court.

Ohio governors face unexpected challenges. In 1985, Governor Celeste was confronted with the unexpected default of the savings and loan industry in Ohio, which led to actual bank closings. Ohio was one of the few states that operated a private insurance fund for savings and loans, and so those banks did not have federal insurance. Governor Voinovich was confronted with inmate riots and the taking of guards as hostages by inmates at the state's Lucasville State Prison.

The Ohio governor has almost unlimited power of clemency. During his first three years in office, Governor Kasich received 1,031 applications for clemency. He approved 51 of those. Clemency can be given in the form of a pardon or a commutation. A pardon is an act that forgives guilt. A commutation focuses on the punishment rather than the offense. When governors use commutation power, they reduce the penalty or sentence that is attached to a conviction. Five of those approved for clemency by Governor Kasich involved the commuting of the death penalty.

Governors and Political Parties

The governor is viewed as the leader of his state party. Governor John Kasich encountered thorny problems with the Ohio GOP. In 2012, despite the courtship by presidential candidates, Kasich did not endorse a candidate; he did speak for the Ohio delegation on behalf of the GOP presidential nominee, Mitt Romney, at the national convention. The Kasich political clique did not think that the state chairman Kevin DeWine gave Kasich the full support of the state party in the 2010 election. In 2013, after a struggle, DeWine was replaced by Matt Borges, a close Kasich ally.

Borges stayed loyal to Kasich throughout Kasich's failed presidential campaign. Kasich would neither attend nor speak at the 2016 Republican National Convention, held in Cleveland, Ohio. In the general election, the Republican nominee, Donald Trump, won Ohio by eight percent. Trump supporters in Ohio, with the encouragement and active participation of Trump himself, successfully moved to replace Kasich ally Borges as state party GOP chair with a Trump ally, Jane Timkin, prior to Trump's inauguration.

The last Democratic governor, Ted Strickland, enjoyed a more normal relationship with his state party. In 2006, gubernatorial candidate Strickland indicated he wanted Chris Redfern to be the state party chair. Redfern was elected chair with little controversy.

Other Executive Offices

There are four separately elected offices in Ohio: the Ohio attorney general, the Ohio secretary of state, the auditor of the state of Ohio, and the treasurer of the state of Ohio. All of these officials are elected in the midterm election year. They are all term limited to two consecutive four-year terms.

These separately elected administrative officials can become problematic for the governor of Ohio. Attorney General Mark Dann, who was elected on the coattails of Governor Ted Strickland in 2006, became an embarrassment to Strickland because of his hiring of questionable associates and overall frat boy antics in Columbus. Governor Strickland threatened to have him impeached and forced his resignation. Governor John Kasich found state treasurer, Josh Mandel, a thorn in his side. Mandel publicly opposed Kasich on a number of budget issues far beyond the jurisdiction of his office including the Medicaid expansion.

The elected attorney general serves as legal counsel for the state. It provides defense of state offices in federal court. There have been numerous challenges to Ohio voting law and regulations particularly in presidential election years and the attorney general provides the legal support for the state's policies. The office provides legal opinions to public entities in the state. A review of recent opinions shows that the county prosecutors make the most frequent requests for opinion. The legal weight of the opinion, while persuasive, is neither conclusive nor binding. Over the years the office has taken on additional duties. One of those is supervision of the Bureau of Criminal Identification (BCI), which was created in 1963. This bureau provides local law enforcement and county prosecutors with modern analytical methods of investigating crimes. Republican Attorney General Mike DeWine frequently joined other Republican attorneys general to challenge many of President Obama's policies, particularly issues surrounding the Affordable Care Act, in federal court.

The most visible public function of the Ohio secretary of state involves supervision of elections. For many years the office was viewed as administrative and not very political. That changed after Bob Taft left the office to serve as governor. He was replaced by Republican Ken Blackwell who was often charged with using the office to issue policies on voting that favored his party. That continued with Secretary of State Jon Husted, who tried to limit early voting in Ohio. His policies were frequently challenged in federal court by the Obama campaign and Husted was forced to reverse many of his early voting directives.

The Ohio auditor is required to conduct post-audits of state agencies and units of local governments. The responsibility is termed *legal-fiscal audits* and the audits determine the legality and propriety of expenditures. Occasional findings are issued against local governments. The auditor has legal power to restrict the financial authority of local governments and school districts if they do not meet certain fiscal measures. The most significant political issue in recent years raised by the state auditor has been over Ohio Department of Education spending for charter schools.

The Ohio auditor's office was once a bastion of political patronage. That changed with the imposition of term limits in 1992 and the move to contract out most services to private firms. It is still viewed as a political prize since it is an office on the state apportionment board.

The office of treasurer is responsible for investing the state's funds for safekeeping and disbursing warrants (checks) in payment for state obligations. This office, like the auditor's office is administrative and not a policy making office. Treasurer Josh Mandel tried to gain publicity by promoting the open checkbook where government expenditures including public employee salaries were made available online.

The Ohio governor has a cabinet of twenty-six departments with varying size and responsibility. The most important agencies for the governor include the Office of Budget and Management. That office puts forward the executive budget and also monitors expenditures; if it appears that the budget is not going to balance at the end of the fiscal year the governor will have to either cut spending or find more revenue, neither of which are attractive political choices, so good budget management has political value. Governor Kasich pushed hard to create JobsOhio, which is funded by the state liquor profits. JobsOhio offers various incentives to attract business to the state and create and retain jobs. JobsOhio offers low interest loans, tax credits, and venture capital. New investment and economic expansion are a key measure of the success of a governor. A board appointed by the governor oversees this not-for-profit agency.

The Ohio Court System

The Ohio court system's roots extend back to the Northwest Ordinance of 1787. The territory covered by the ordinance was to be administered by a governor working with three judges. Although the judges were empowered to hear cases, they also served as quasi-legislators. Acting in that capacity, the second law that they approved formed what was called a court of common pleas, a term that is still used in Ohio. The law called for the appointing of between three and five judges in each county to this newly formed court. From those humble beginnings has evolved a complex court system that includes more than 720 elected judges who collectively process nearly three million cases each year.[31]

The threshold of the Ohio court system is a series of trial courts. These include municipal courts, county courts, common pleas courts, and even

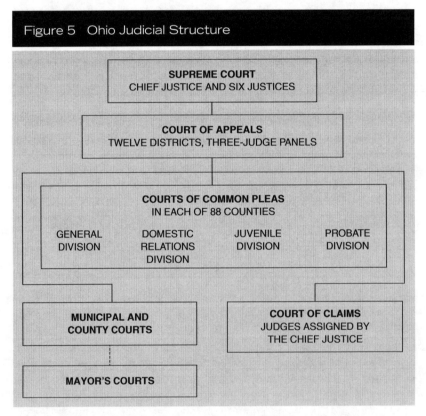

Figure 5   Ohio Judicial Structure

SUPREME COURT
CHIEF JUSTICE AND SIX JUSTICES

COURT OF APPEALS
TWELVE DISTRICTS, THREE-JUDGE PANELS

COURTS OF COMMON PLEAS
IN EACH OF 88 COUNTIES

GENERAL DIVISION   DOMESTIC RELATIONS DIVISION   JUVENILE DIVISION   PROBATE DIVISION

MUNICIPAL AND COUNTY COURTS

COURT OF CLAIMS
JUDGES ASSIGNED BY THE CHIEF JUSTICE

MAYOR'S COURTS

Source: Website of the Supreme Court of Ohio and the Ohio Judicial System.

mayor's courts. With a few exceptions, almost all cases in Ohio originate in one of these trial courts. Those who lose at the trial court level may appeal their case to an intermediate appeals court, known in Ohio as the court of appeals.[32] Finally, the court of last resort in Ohio is called the supreme court. The one unique feature of the Ohio court system—shared only by Louisiana—is that Ohio allows mayors in certain towns and cities to hold what are called mayor's courts. These courts are presided over by a mayor who is not required to have a law degree. He or she is required to receive specific training, and usually hears cases involving the violation of local ordinances and traffic laws.

Magistrates

The late chief justice of the Ohio Supreme Court, Thomas Moyer, said that magistrates "are the face of the [Ohio] judiciary."[33] In Ohio, magistrates, who before 1990 were called referees, perform activities normally associated with judges, such as conducting pre-trial hearings, setting bail, and even conducting nonjury trials. Although magistrates can issue orders—for example, granting a continuance in a case—they cannot issue final judgments, and a judge must adopt decisions that they make before they become effective.

Judges at every court level in Ohio have the power to appoint magistrates. In order to be qualified to serve, an individual is required to have practiced law for at least four years. There is no set term or salary for magistrates. Currently more than eight hundred magistrates work in the Ohio court system. Magistrates may serve in more than one court, and in several counties at the same time.

Mayor's Courts

Municipal corporations in Ohio with populations greater than two hundred may establish what are called a mayor's court. A mayor's court is only empowered to hear cases involving local ordinances and state traffic offenses. Local mayors who preside over these courts are not required to be lawyers, but must receive some legal training. Currently, 297 municipal corporations in Ohio have a mayor's court. In 2016, these courts had an overall caseload that was just under 300,000 cases.[34] Over three-quarters of these cases involved traffic violations. Since most potential cases are terminated by the accused simply paying a fine to the local traffic bureau, only 1,302 actual trials occurred in mayor's courts in 2016. Mayors themselves conducted 128 of these trials, with the remainder being presided over by magistrates.[35]

Municipal and County Courts

There are 35 county courts and 129 municipal courts in Ohio. These courts are the workhorses of the Ohio court system.[36] In 2016, municipal courts were responsible for over 2.1 million cases, while county courts heard an additional 163,627 cases.[37] Both municipal and county courts are the creation of the Ohio legislature, relying on its power under Article IV of the State Constitution to create inferior courts (that is, courts that are below the Ohio Supreme Court, court of appeals, and common pleas courts). In some counties, the state has only allowed for municipal courts, while in other counties, county courts have been authorized for geographical areas not covered by municipal courts. The jurisdiction (kinds of cases that a court may hear) of municipal and county courts is identical. These courts are empowered to hear criminal misdemeanor cases, traffic cases, and civil actions where the amount of money involved is less than $15,000. County court judges in Ohio serve part-time, while municipal court judges may be either full-time or part-time.

Courts of Common Pleas

Unlike the municipal and county courts, the court of common pleas of Ohio is established directly by the Ohio Constitution and is the trial court that hears most serious cases in Ohio. Each of the eighty-eight counties has a court of common pleas. In most counties the court is divided into criminal and civil, domestic relations, probate, and juvenile divisions. The criminal and civil divisions handle criminal felony cases, and civil cases involving more than $15,000. The domestic relations division of the courts of common pleas hears marriage-related cases, such as divorces, legal separations, and annulments. Judges assigned to the juvenile division of the courts of common pleas have exclusive jurisdiction over cases involving those under the age of 18, including cases where adults are accused of contributing to the delinquency of minors. Finally, the probate division is responsible for making determinations about wills and estates, as well as determining such issues as legal guardianships and adoptions. The probate division also issues marriage licenses.

Courts of Appeals

Those who are unhappy with the decision made at the municipal, county, or common pleas court level may appeal the decision to the court of appeals in their districts. There are the twelve courts of appeals, each representing a district that encompasses between one and seventeen counties. The legislature establishes the districts and also determines, based on both population and caseload, the number of judges who will serve in each of the districts. The districts are not equal in population. The 4th District, for example, encompasses 633,838 people, while the 5th District is twice as large, with a population of 1,484,932. Currently, there are at least four and as many as twelve judges on each appeals court.

Courts of appeals in Ohio exercise both appellate jurisdiction (the ability to hear a case on appeal from a lower court) and original jurisdiction (the ability to hear a case before any other court has rendered a decision). The court of appeals may exercise its original jurisdiction in cases where a party is seeking a writ of quo warranto (questioning a public official's right to their office or powers), mandamus (commanding a public official to perform a duty), habeas corpus (determining whether a prisoner is being legally held), prohibition (ordering a halt to proceedings beyond a lower court's legal authority), or procedendo (order to a lower court to proceed to a judgment), and, according to Article IV, section 3 of the Ohio Constitution, "[i]n any cause on review as may be necessary to its complete determination." These types of cases are rare, however, and compose a very small percentage of the cases heard by courts of appeals in Ohio. On average, nearly half of the cases heard by courts of appeals are appeals of lower court decisions in criminal cases.

Regardless of how many judges are on an individual court of appeals, randomly selected panels made up of only three of the judges hear cases. A court of appeals may issue several different types of decisions. The court may, for example, decide to overturn or uphold a decision made by a lower court. Alternatively, a court of appeals may determine that the decision of a lower court needs to be modified or that additional proceedings need to take place.

The Ohio Supreme Court

The Supreme Court of Ohio is the court of last resort in the Buckeye state. Formally established by Article IV, section 2 of the Ohio Constitution, the court has, since 1913, consisted of six justices and one chief justice. When deciding cases, the chief justice's vote carries no more weight than the vote of the remaining six justices. The chief justice does, however, have some additional administrative responsibilities, including appointing judges to the court of claims or to other courts when necessary.

Like the courts of appeals, the Ohio Supreme Court is primarily a court of appellate jurisdiction. The supreme court's limited original jurisdiction mirrors that of the courts of appeals discussed above. The only difference is that the supreme court is also empowered to hear, within its original jurisdiction, cases involving the practice of law, including disciplinary cases against lawyers.

The supreme court primarily hears cases that are brought to it from the courts of appeal. Under the Ohio Constitution, although the supreme court has discretion over which criminal and civil cases it chooses to hear, the court is required to grant review to the following cases: (1) cases that originate in the court of appeals, (2) cases in which the death penalty was affirmed, or (3) cases which involve a federal or state constitutional question. The court must also hear appeals from certain administrative agencies. In addition to deciding cases, the supreme court is responsible for adopting rules governing the Ohio courts.

In 2016, 1,914 cases were appealed to the supreme court. Of these cases, 1,382 were what are called jurisdictional appeals, meaning that the supreme court could decide whether or not to hear these cases. The court granted full review to 75 (or about four percent) of these appeals.[38]

The supreme court normally hears cases in the state capital of Columbus. Since 1987, however, as part of the Off-Site Court Program, the Ohio Supreme Court holds hearings twice a year in different counties around the state. The court hears arguments on Tuesday and Wednesday mornings, with formal written opinions also being announced on Wednesdays. A lottery system is used to determine which justice (including the chief justice) will be assigned to write the opinion that represents a majority (at least four members) of the court. Numbered balls, corresponding to each of the justices voting with the majority—and the chief justice, if she is part of the majority—are placed in a bottle with a top narrow enough to allow only one ball at a time to escape. The justice who voted with the majority who has served on the court for the longest period of time (the "senior justice") tilts the bottle to release a ball. The justice, or chief justice, whose number corresponds with the number on the ball, is assigned to write the opinion. So that all of the justices are assigned a similar number of opinions, that numbered ball is not reused until everyone on the court has been assigned an opinion.[39]

Court of Claims

The Ohio General Assembly created the Court of Claims in 1975. The court of claims hears cases involving civil claims against the State of Ohio. Unlike other courts in Ohio, the court of claims does not have permanent judges. The court does have a clerk and deputy clerk, and these officials decide cases where claims are in the amount of $10,000 or less. If the decision of clerk or deputy clerk is appealed, or if the amount in question is more than $10,000, either a judge or a panel of judges (in very complex cases) appointed by the chief justice of the Ohio Supreme Court hears the case.

The Court of Claims also hears appeals from the decisions of the Ohio Attorney General's Office in cases where claims have been made under the Victims of Crimes Act. The chief justice also appoints a panel of three commissioners who hear the initial appeals in these cases. The commissioners serve six-year terms. A final appeal from a decision by the commissioners may be taken to a Court of Claims judge.

Judicial Selection in Ohio

Under the state's first constitution, judges in Ohio were to be elected by the General Assembly. When, in 1851, a new constitution was adopted, it made several changes to Ohio judiciary, including providing for the popular election of judges. Ohio is now one of twenty-one states that allow voters to select their judges at the polls.[40]

Although Ohio has elected its judges for more than 160 years, the process has undergone some changes. Originally, the political parties nominated judges through various methods, including party conventions. The party affiliation of the judge was then listed on the general election ballot. In 1911, the General Assembly passed the Nonpartisan Judiciary Act, which ordered the party affiliation of judges to be removed from the ballot.[41] The next year, the Ohio Constitution was amended to mandate that the political parties use primaries to select their standard bearers. In practice, this means that judges in Ohio are selected in partisan political primaries, and therefore generally must run as Democrats or Republicans. General election voters, however, are not provided with any information on the ballot about the political affiliation of the judicial candidates nominated by the parties. Now, because judges are expected to decide cases in a nonpartisan manner, the use of nonpartisan ballots is not unusual in the United States. Among the states that elect judges, all but seven ban the inclusion of party affiliation on the ballot. Ohio is the only state, however, that combines a nonpartisan general election ballot with a partisan primary election system.

The judges and justices, including the chief justice of the Ohio Supreme Court, are elected to six-year terms. Municipal court judges are elected during odd numbered years, while all other judges appear on the ballot in even numbered years. All judges, including the chief justice and justices of the Supreme Court, can be removed from office by a vote of two-thirds of both houses of the General Assembly. If a vacancy occurs on any court, the governor is empowered to make a temporary appointment.

A recent survey by the Bliss Institute at the University of Akron showed that a majority of Ohio registered voter respondents (fifty-six percent) thought that "it was likely that unqualified people are elected as judges" in Ohio.[42] There are serious questions about how much information voters have about judicial candidates. This lack of information may lead to what is sometimes called the "name game" when it comes to elections for the Ohio Supreme Court. For example, over the past fifty years, seven different members of the Ohio Supreme Court have shared the last surname "Brown."[43] Because of this, there have been several attempts to amend the Ohio Constitution to change how judicial selection takes place in Ohio. These revisions often call for gubernatorial appointments from a list of candidates prescreened by an independent panel. This method, called "merit selection," was proposed as a constitutional amendment in 1938. The proposed amendment called for all appellate court judges (judges on the courts of appeals and justices and the chief justice of the Ohio Supreme Court) to be nominated by the governor from among a slate of individuals recommended by an eight-member judicial council. The nominations would be subject to a confirmation vote in the senate. After a term in office, judges would have to go before the voters in a retention election. There would be no opponent, and the voters would only be casting their ballots on the question of whether to retain the judge in office.

Ohio voters overwhelmingly rejected the 1938 amendment. In the years since, many plans were put forward in Ohio similar to the merit plan of 1938. In 1968, voters in Ohio approved what was summarized as "The Modern Courts Amendment." The amendment made several additions to the Ohio Constitution, for example, strengthening the leadership role of the Ohio Supreme Court over other courts in the state.[44] Originally, the proposed set of changes included a merit selection provision. The Ohio House of Representatives removed this provision before the ballot measure was placed before the voters.[45] The most recent serious attempt to change how judges are selected in Ohio took place in 1987, when a proposal was placed on the Ohio ballot that would have established merit panels for each of the appellate districts and the state supreme court. As in the 1938 proposal, these panels would have recommended candidates for nomination by the governor. The near 2–1 margin of defeat for the 1987 ballot measure was nearly identical to the 1938 vote.[46] More recently, a poll showed that over eighty percent of Ohioans want to keep voting for judges, or at least supreme court justices.[47]

Finally, despite all the discussions about judicial elections, more than half of the judges serving in Ohio first gain their position by gubernatorial appointment. Given the natural advantage that incumbents have on the ballot, this represents a rather important and unchecked power granted to the Ohio governor.

Political Parties and Participation

Ohio has a history of strong political parties. The Ohio Democratic Party is older than the Republican Party, having its origins in the founding period of the state. Initially, a party known as the Federalists served as the main rival to the Democratic Party (or the Democratic or Jeffersonian Republicans, as they were known). As the Federalist Party faded, the Whig party emerged as the opponents of the Democrats.[48] The Whigs were strong in the northeast corner or "Western Reserve" part of Ohio. The Ohio Whig party held strong abolitionist views, and served as part of the core of the party realignment that occurred with the emergence of the Republican Party in Ohio in the 1850s.

"Third" Parties in Ohio

Beyond the Democrats and the Republicans, minor, or so-called third parties, have struggled to gain ballot access and sustain their legal status in Ohio. In the 2016 general election, Libertarian Gary Johnson, for example, (although forced to run without any party label) garnered only a little over three percent of the total vote in Ohio.

Even though third parties do not currently have much hope for winning the plurality of the votes necessary to actually be awarded an office in Ohio, they can affect a close election by siphoning off votes that might otherwise go to one of the major party candidates. For this reason, it is sometimes said there is only one thing Ohio Republicans and Democrats agree on: making it difficult for third parties to gain ballot access.

Prior to 2006, Ohio law required minor parties to collect signatures equivalent to one percent of the total vote cast in the most recent statewide election in order to have their candidate's name placed on the ballot. These signatures had to be submitted 120 days prior to the primary election. Once they appeared on the ballot, the minor party's gubernatorial candidate (or slate of electors in a presidential year) had to attract at least five percent of the total votes cast. If the party failed to cross the five percent threshold, they had to start all over again to gain ballot access.

In response to a legal challenge brought by the Libertarian Party of Ohio, a federal court declared those requirements unconstitutional in 2006.[49] The result was that it became easy for minor parties to gain ballot access. In the period from 2006 to 2013, the Green Party, the Libertarian Party, Constitution Party, the Socialist Party, and the American Election Party all gained access to Ohio's ballot. Ohio also established that if two or more candidates filed for the nomination for the same office of the same minor party, the state would conduct a primary election.[50]

In November of 2013, the Republican-controlled General Assembly passed a new ballot access measure for minor political parties. The new law requires minor parties to collect one-half of one percent of the vote cast in the last presidential election in order to be recognized on the ballot. That was estimated to be about 28,000 signatures, with the requirement that at least 500 of the signatures have to come from eight of the sixteen congressional districts in the state.

The Tea Party movement, unhappy with John Kasich for the Medicaid expansion, decided to give its support to former State Representative Charlie Earl who was to be the Libertarian candidate for governor. The Libertarians gained relief in federal court against more restrictive requirements. Still, under rules promulgated by the Ohio secretary of state, minor party candidates face signature requirements similar to those applied to major party candidates. In 2014, Secretary of State Jon Husted determined that Libertarian gubernatorial candidate Charlie Earl and his running mate Sherry Clark had violated these requirements and therefore could not appear on the primary ballot. Consequently, they were also barred from appearing on the 2014 general election ballot. That was viewed as a goal of the Kasich gubernatorial re-election campaign.

Governing Parties

Ohio State law offers very limited regulation of its political parties beyond minor party status as discussed above. The Ohio Revised Code (ORC) says that "The controlling committees of each major political party shall be a state committee consisting of two members, one male and one female, elected every two years from each of the 33 Senate districts."[51] That means that there are sixty-six members of each party's state committee. Ohio statute also speaks to county central committees; one member is elected from each precinct or from each ward and township in the county. These state and local committees are elected in the primaries in even years. After the primary, they meet to organize by adopting by-laws and party chairs.

The Ohio state law on party organization and function is very thin because political parties are private, nongovernmental organizations. The strictest regulations governing political parties in Ohio are in the area of campaign finance law.

Some of these state or county party committees might choose to endorse candidates in the primary. Those endorsements carry none of the benefits sometimes found in other states, such as automatic ballot access or preferred position on the primary ballot. The value of a party endorsement in Ohio is dependent on the support the endorsing party organization invests in it. In recent election cycles the endorsement of the Franklin County Republican Party has contributed to winnowing out statewide candidates.

The most significant statutory authority granted to county committees in Ohio is the power to replace partisan-elected office holders who have vacated (or been removed) from their offices in the county. The power does not extend to judges, who are nominated in party primaries. State statutes empower the governor to fill vacant judicial positions at all levels. When a state legislator leaves before his term is up, the respective party caucuses in the House or Senate replace them. The governor fills vacancies in other statewide administrative offices.

Legislative Party Committees

There are other nonstatutory party organizations in Ohio. The most important are the legislative party committees. The legislative caucuses for each party select the members of these committees. These committees hire staff and often a consulting firm to support them. Their function is to recruit and elect candidates for the next election cycle. This is an arduous task whose difficulty is compounded by term limits. Term limits create numerous open seats, and the legislative campaign committee is expected to recruit viable candidates in those districts deemed competitive. Recruiting legislative candidates is challenging. The best prospects are those who hold some sort of local office in the district and are able to raise some campaign funds or self-finance some of their own campaign. Another pool of candidates are former legislators who have been or are going to be termed out of office. The caucus campaign committees are also expected to raise funds to support those candidates newly recruited as well as provide support to incumbents at risk. This practice is termed *targeting*. Targeting is a practice of legislative campaign committees, political parties, and political action committees (PACs), which focus scarce financial resources on either candidates that have a good chance of winning or on incumbents that appear vulnerable. In an Ohio state house election, the number of contested seats, where both parties are financially engaged, is usually less than a dozen.

Parties and the Political Environment

John Fenton, in his 1966 book, *Midwest Politics,* places his study of Ohio politics in a section titled "The Jobs Oriented States." According to Fenton, "the distinguishing characteristic of jobs-oriented politics is that most of the people who participate in politics on a day-to-day basis do so out of a desire for jobs or contracts rather than because of a concern for public policy."[52] That description would not capture today's Ohio political parties. A variety of factors have eroded the patronage available to Ohio parties, including implementation of civil service law, the onset of public sector unions, outsourcing of state work to private contractors, and the effect of the 1990 supreme court decision *Rutan et al. v. Republican Party of Illinois.* In *Rutan,* the court essentially made patronage illegal, ruling that state governments violate an individual's First Amendment rights when they hire (or refuse to hire), fire, or promote state employees on the basis of political affiliation or party activity. Even if patronage jobs were still available, there would not be many of them. All recent governors have bragged they have reduced the number of state workers. The push to privatize state work has reduced the number of public employees and changed the nature of patronage.

One of Fenton's chapters was titled "Issueless Politics in Ohio." In fact, the long-serving, well-respected Republican state party chairman at the time, Ray Bliss, was noted for keeping issues out of state politics. Instead, he focused on building a strong party organization. As Fenton noted, Republicans "constituted a minority of the voting population of the state and were willing to submit to strong central direction of their party in order to achieve electoral victory over a disorganized majority."[53]

The reluctance to bring up controversial issues no longer describes today's Ohio Republican Party; the large Republican majorities in the Ohio House tried to strip public unions of their closed shop benefits and lost in the statewide referendum in 2011. Governor Kasich expanded Medicaid, without the support of the Republican dominated Ohio General Assembly. Republicans offer legislation restricting abortions and expanding gun rights in every legislative session. The Ohio GOP has also become a strong advocate of charter schools.

The most recent divisions in the Ohio Republican Party are a result of Governor John Kasich's 2016 presidential bid, and his reluctance to support presidential candidate and now President Donald Trump. The impact of the rift on the 2018 Ohio election is not yet evident, but it did result in the ouster of Ohio GOP state chair Matt Borges, with the Trump camp supporter, Jane Timken, in a very close vote of the state committee.

In the 1960s, according to Fenton there was not a statewide Democratic Party, there was an aggregation of urban city machines. The city party bosses were not interested in winning statewide office unless the candidate was from their town. That changed with the rise of Ohio House Speaker Vernal Riffe who served from 1975 until 1995. He used his position to raise funds for the Ohio Democratic Party. He was also influential in the nomination and election of Ohio Democratic Governor Dick Celeste, who served from 1983 until 1991. With the support of Speaker Riffe the Democrats enacted much of their agenda including collective bargaining rights for public employees. A state income tax increase in the Celeste years cost the Democrats the Ohio senate and they have never regained control of that body. The unions in Ohio were very influential in Ohio Democratic Party politics but their influence has waned with deindustrialization in Ohio.

All office seekers who wish to run as a major party candidate in Ohio must seek the party nomination in a primary. A *primary* is an election held before the general election to nominate a political party's candidate for office. Primaries replaced caucuses (meetings of party members) as a means to nominate candidates early in Ohio history. Direct primaries were mandated for elective offices in 1912. Ohio uses what is known as a *semi-closed* primary. In Ohio, a voter is permitted to change party affiliation or declare for a particular party on the day of the primary.

Ohio uses a plurality electoral system; the candidate who receives the most votes, whether or not that amounts to a majority of the votes cast, will be the party nominee. Normally the Ohio primary is the first Tuesday after the first Monday in May. In 2016, that was changed to mid-March to accommodate the presidential campaign of John Kasich. National party rules required a later date if the state party wanted to use winner-take-all for convention delegates. Ohio was the only state Kasich won and he took all the Ohio GOP delegates, but he did not attend the Republican National Convention.

For general elections, Ohio follows the federal pattern of holding the election on the first Tuesday after the first Monday of November. In keeping with a 1949 state constitutional amendment, Ohio employs what is called an *office-bloc ballot*. This means that the names of candidates are listed under the office they are seeking. Party designation is listed under the name of the candidate. The 1949 amendment abolished the old *straight ticket* arrangement, where candidates' names are arranged by party. With a few exceptions, township trustees and school boards, Ohio uses single member district plurality elections; that is, only one office holder is elected from a district, and the candidate who receives the most votes wins.

Elections in Ohio are conducted by the eighty-eight county Election Boards, which are organized by state statute. Each county has a board of elections with two Democratic members and two Republican members. They are nominated by the local party committees and appointed by the secretary of state for a four-year term. It is customary for the local county party chairs to have seats on this board and receive the modest pay. The system is designed as a checks and balances; the Democrats are to keep an eye on the Republican workers and vice versa. The board selects the type of technology that is used for voting and the counting of votes, if approved by the secretary of state. In the case of a tie on the county board, the secretary of state breaks the tie.

In order to be able to vote in Ohio a person is to register thirty days before the election. In the general election of 2016, there were 5,607,641 votes cast; of those thirty-three percent or 1,879,630 were not cast at the precinct level on election day. Of those 665,461 were cast in person. These voters have become known as early votes. In 2005, Ohio adopted "no-fault" absentee voting; that is, an excuse of some sort such as sickness or absent from the county or age is no longer required. No reason needs to be offered. In the same law was the opportunity for voters to cast their ballots at the board of elections or other designated locations before Election Day. This was called *early in person (EIP) voting*. A study by the Bliss Institute of Politics at the University of Akron found that the demographic characteristics of these early voters were more likely to be women, older, and of lower education and income. Perhaps more importantly, these voters favored Democrats.[54] Early voting has led to a number of partisan disputes that were taken to federal court. The first issue was what was called "golden week." The initial law permitted early voting to begin thirty-five days prior to an election. Voters are allowed to register to vote up to thirty days before an election. The result was a five-day so-called golden week, during which someone could, on the same day, both register to vote and actually cast a vote. That was challenged in the legislature and in federal court. The other issue raised by early voting is the opportunity to vote on the Sunday before election day. The Republican secretary of state issued administrative rules limiting that opportunity and that has been challenged in court. Perhaps one reason early voting rules have been so litigious in Ohio is because Ohio is viewed as a battleground state.

Local Government in Ohio

Local government in Ohio has its origins in the Land Ordinance of 1785. Passed by the continental Congress to prepare for the sale of this land, this ordinance proposed surveying the western lands into six square mile townships. In the Ohio territory, a five-mile square was often substituted for the six-mile square township. In 1804, after Ohio became a state, the General Assembly decided to create civil townships throughout Ohio. When the population of the townships reached eighty, the residents could form a township government. The powers and duties of townships decreased over the decades as more and more counties were created by the Ohio legislature. Local political subdivisions in Ohio now include counties, townships, villages, and cities.

Counties

The state of Ohio gradually increased the number of county governments until it reached the current number of eighty-eight. The county is an agent of state government and the state statutes specifically spell out the structure and the duties of the counties. There are three elected commissioners in each county in Ohio. Two commissioners are elected in the year of the presidential election and one is elected in the mid-term election. They are elected for four-year terms and have legislative and executive authority. The authority of the commissioners is limited by state statute and by the fact that there are numerous separately elected county officials including prosecutor, sheriff, auditor, coroner, treasurer, clerk of courts, county engineer, and the county recorder. This county form of government is seen as outdated and inefficient by reformers in Ohio. County government relies on the piggyback sales tax for most of its revenue. *Piggyback* means that the county sales tax is on top of the state sales tax and is collected with it. The lion's share of Ohio's county government budgets goes to public safety, which includes the sheriff's department, the courts, and the county jail. That is usually seventy percent of an Ohio county's own-source revenue.

Townships

There are 1,308 townships in Ohio and they provide limited local government services for citizens who do not reside in an incorporated municipality. The Ohio Constitution provides for a township government and for the General Assembly to provide for its form and powers of general law. Townships can only exercise those powers delegated to them by the General Assembly. A three-member board of trustees governs townships. Two are elected on one odd year and the third is elected in the next odd year. Trustees enjoy a four-year term in office and may be reelected. Trustees have both legislative and executive authority, although it is quite limited and prescribed by state law. The township fiscal officer is also elected every four years. These local officials are elected in nonpartisan elections.

The only own-source revenue for these townships is the property tax. Additional property tax has to be voted for by the residents. Townships have very limited authority. They have basic functions such as road maintenance, operating a cemetery, fire protection, and zoning (if adopted by the residents). The governments can provide for police protection if they provide the needed financial support by voting for a levy, otherwise the responsibility for policing defaults to the county. More populated Ohio townships do not seek to incorporate since many functions performed by the county would become the responsibility of the incorporated municipality.

Municipalities

According to the U.S. Census of Governments, there are 938 municipalities in Ohio. This includes cities and villages both chartered and statutory. The authority of municipal government in Ohio is defined by Article XVIII of the state constitution, which was initiated by the Ohio Constitutional Convention of 1912. Article XVIII states, "Municipalities shall have authority to exercise all powers of local government and to adopt and enforce within their limits such local police, sanitary and other similar regulations, as are not in conflict with general laws."

Incorporated municipalities can take multiple paths for self-governance. They can adopt the statutory form. That is the local government form prescribed by Ohio statute. That form most frequently provides for a strong mayor/council organization for Ohio cities and a weak mayor council plan for villages. An incorporated village becomes a city if its population exceeds five thousand.

The charter is a legal instrument that resembles a constitution for the municipal government. The charter does not expand the scope of municipal power, but it does provide the opportunity to be responsive to local needs rather than rely on the General Assembly, as is the case with the statutory form. As of 1995, there were 173 cities and 51 villages with charters in Ohio.

The population of all but one of Ohio's major cities declined from the census of 2000 to the census of 2010. Those cities include Akron, Cincinnati, Cleveland, Dayton, and Toledo. The only city to grow was the city that is home to the state capital of Ohio, Columbus. That city's population increased from 711,470 in 2000 to 787,033, in 2010, making it the largest city in the state. Columbus has grown because it has pursued annexation: its boundaries now extend beyond the boundaries of its home county, Franklin County. It pursued this expansion by refusing to provide water and sewer services unless the neighboring jurisdictions seeking those services agreed to annex to the City of Columbus. Annexation is a legal process by which some property in an unincorporated area such as a township becomes part of a neighboring city or village. The property needs to be contiguous to qualify for annexation. The most common scenario is that the property owner will seek to have the property annexed. The city of Columbus maintained tight control over its water and sewer services according to Columbus Mayor Buck Rinehart. One notable example of the expansion of the city boundary of Columbus is the privately developed Polaris Centers of Commerce, which expands into Delaware County, Ohio, and was annexed to Columbus to acquire water and sewer services. Columbus annexed it during the construction of the privately funded interchanges on Interstate 71.

The grant of home rule to incorporated municipalities under Ohio Constitution Article XVIII has continually been litigated in Ohio courts. There are often questions regarding the authority of an Ohio city that has a charter and has adopted by ordinance or charter amendment that appears to be in conflict with a state statute. A recent legal challenge to home rule involved an incorporated city's authority to require their police officers to reside inside the city limits. This requirement was at odds with a recently enacted state statute that permitted noncity residents to serve as police officers. The trial court supported the plaintiff's effort to overturn the city's residency requirement. The appellate court overturned the trial court's decision. In the end, former Justice Paul Pfeifer writing for the majority of the Ohio Supreme Court concluded that validly enacted state statutes (prevailed) over conflicting local laws.[55]

Ohio law allows for the creation of special districts that are governed by an appointed board. The U.S. Census Bureau reported that there were seven hundred such special districts in Ohio in 2012. These districts usually have a single purpose and often have their own revenue source. This revenue source is usually a property tax; however, some county transit authorities are permitted to have a piggyback on their state and county sales tax. In Ohio, enabling statutes create and dictate the form of special districts. For example, port authorities might be created by municipal ordinance or township or county resolution. A regional water and sewer district is created by order of the court of common pleas upon granting the petition of one or more political subdivisions.[56] The special districts can span part of a county or span a number of counties. A few examples of the types of special districts in Ohio include a county library district, a water district, a park district, a joint fire district, a sanitary district, a soil and water conservation district, or a regional airport. Frequently these districts are in response to a demand and a lack of mergers of local governments in Ohio municipal history.[57]

Ohio has diminished its financial support to its local governments. The state of Ohio provides direct support to its local governments through the local government fund (LGF), which is allocated to counties and then divided up among the various political subdivisions. In 1972, the state added a new element allowing municipalities to receive share of LGF. The LGF has existed in Ohio since 1934, when the state passed a three percent sales tax; one of the purposes was to support local government activities. In 1935, local governments received forty percent of the monies generated by the sales tax after certain expenses were met.[58] In his first year in office Governor John Kasich was confronted with an $8 billion shortfall for fiscal year (FY) 2012–2013 budget. Kasich in an effort to cut the budget imposed the largest cut on local government, by cutting the LGF by twenty-five percent in FY 2012 and fifty percent by 2013. In those state budgets, the LFG amount was no longer expressed as a percentage of tax receipts but as a fixed dollar amount. The FY 2014–2015 budget while incorporating the fifty percent cut in permanent law, went back to expressing the amount in terms of the percentage of the taxes collected that would be dedicated to the LGF. There were additional cuts to local government and schools with the phasing out of the tangible personal property tax. Over recent decades, Ohio's support for its governments has been on the decline. The degree of state oversight and regulation of local governments has been on the increase.

The Ohio Budget

Ohio is one of the few large governmental units that uses a biennial budget. There is some merit to a two-year budget because it reduces the conflict over the budget to every other year. Ohio adopts two separate annual budgets that are in balance each fiscal year. The fiscal year (FY) starts on July 1. One challenge for such a lengthy budget is accurate revenue forecasts. Although forecasts have been off in past budget cycles, the FY 17 was on target. Ohio also carries forward a surplus. That surplus amounted to $2,034,051,458.[59] Officially called the stabilization fund, it is known as the "rainy day fund" and is regularly pointed to as a revenue source by interest groups seeking funding. Governor Kasich has been adamant about not spending these funds and points to it as evidence of the success of his government.

Ohio has a variety of revenue sources. The largest is federal grants, which account for thirty-four percent of its revenue. Most of that is Medicaid funds, which is a categorical grant.

The largest source of own-source revenue is the sales and use tax, which is thirty-one percent of the state's revenue. That tax is now at 5.75 percent. That is followed by the personal income tax, a progressive tax, which has been reduced over recent budgets. The tax rate for the highest bracket is 4.997 percent. Other taxes account for eleven percent of the state's revenue. One of those taxes, the severance tax, generated a small amount of money, $11.2 million. Governor Kasich in a series of state budgets has called for an increase in that tax, especially when fracking was booming in Ohio. His efforts to have the General Assembly increase that tax have been unsuccessful. Casino tax revenue, which is distributed primarily to local governments was reported in 2016 to be $270,376,946.

The largest expenditure for Ohio in FY 17 was Medicaid at fifty percent. The second largest expenditure was for primary and secondary education at twenty-three percent, higher education was at 6.7 percent, followed by corrections.

DISCUSSION QUESTIONS

1. Why does Ohio receive so much attention in presidential elections?

2. Identify some major differences between the 1802 Constitution and the 1851 Constitution.

3. What is "gerrymandering"? How might it be affected by the 2015 amendment to the Ohio Constitution?

4. Describe the ways in which Ohio allows for direct democracy.

5. Why is it that the adage "one to meet, twice to win" for Ohio governors is no longer true?

6. How and why does Ohio's method of electing judges differ from the majority of states?

7. Ohio was once known for having "issue-less politics." Is this still an accurate way to characterize politics in the Buckeye State?

NOTES

1. "The States Where Clinton and Trump Are Advertising the Most until Election Day," *Adage,* October 21, 2016, accessed December 2, 2017, http://adage.com/article/campaign-trail/states-where-trump-clinton-spending-most-on-advertising/306377/.

2. California was once considered a competitive state, and some analysts suspect that, as its percentage of Hispanic voters increases, Texas will lose its status as a solid red state.

3. Thomas A. Flinn, "The Outline of Ohio's Politics," *Western Political Quarterly,* Vol. 13 (1960), 702–21.

4. Ibid., 702.

5. John H. Fenton, *Midwest Politics* (New York: Holt, Rinehart and Winston, 1966), 118.

6. Michael Barone and Richard E. Cohen, *The Almanac of American Politics, 2010* (Washington, DC: National Journal Group, 2009), 1155.

7. Carrington T. Marshall, *A History of the Courts and Lawyers of Ohio* (New York: American Historical Society, 1934), 9.

8. Marshall, 34.

9. Transcript of the Northwest Ordinance (1787), http://www.ourdocuments.gov/doc.php?flash=true&doc=8&page=transcript.

10. Ibid.

11. David M. Gold, *Democracy in Session: A History of the Ohio General Assembly* (Athens, OH: Ohio University Press, 2009), 6.

12. G. Alan Tarr, "The Ohio Constitution of 1802: An Introduction" (Rutgers Univ. Center for State Constitutional Studies, 2000).

13. Fred J. Blue, "The Date of Ohio Statehood," *Ohio Academy of History Newsletter* (Autumn 2002), 1.

14. Tarr.

15. Marshall, 94.

16. Ibid., 104.

17. Ibid., 107.

18. Isaac Franklin Patterson, in "The Proposed Constitution of 1874," *The Constitutions of Ohio* (Cleveland: The Arthur H. Clark Co., 1912), 182–236.

19. Barbara A. Terzian, "Ohio's Constitutional Conventions and Constitutions," in *The History of Ohio Law,* ed. Michael Les Benedict and John F. Winkler (Athens: Ohio University Press, 2004), 62–63.

20. Ibid., 63–65.

21. "10-Year Committee to Streamline Ohio Constitution Ends Work 4 Years Early; Critics Say There's Little to Show," *Cleveland.com,* July 21, 2017, accessed November 27, 2017, http://www.cleveland.com/metro/index .ssf/2017/07/ambituous_ohio_constitution_re.html.

22. Vernal Riffe, *Whatever's Fair: The Political Biography of Ohio Speaker Vern Riffe* (Kent, OH: Kent State University Press, 2007).

23. Ohio Legislative Services Commission, *A Guidebook for Ohio Legislators,* 39.

24. Ibid., 47–48.

25. Paul Sracic and William Binning, *Ohio Government and Politics* (Washington, DC: CQ Press, 2016), 123.

26. "Fair Districts Campaign to Press on as Lawmakers Begin Negotiating Redistricting Plan," Gongwer, November 3, 2017.

27. Thad L. Beyle, "Being Governor," in *The State of the States,* ed. Carl Van Horn (Washington, DC: Congressional Quarterly Press, 1993), 79–114.

28. John J. Gargan, "The Ohio Executive Branch," in *Ohio Politics,* ed. Alexander Lamis and Brian Usher, 2nd ed. (Kent, OH: Kent State University Press, 2007), 399–401.

29. David E. Sturrock, Michael Margolis, John C. Green, and Dick Kimmins, "Ohio Elections and Politics in the 1990s," in *Ohio Politics,* 2nd ed., 488.

30. Ibid.

31. Ohio Supreme Court, *Ohio Courts Statistical Summary 2016,* 5, http://www .sconet.state.oh.us/Publications/annrep/16OCSR/summary/2016OCS.pdf.

32. Appeals from a mayor's court would go to the municipal or county court, rather than to the courts of appeals.

33. Chief Justice Thomas Moyer, "Address at New Magistrate Orientation," March 24, 2010.

34. Ohio Supreme Court, *2016 Mayor's Courts Summary*, 7, http://www .supremecourt.ohio.gov/Publications/mayorscourt/mayorscourtreport16.pdf.

35. Ibid.

36. *Ohio Courts Statistical Summary 2016*, 5.

37. Ibid., 7.

38. Ibid., 10.

39. Ohio Supreme Court, "The Supreme Court of Ohio and the Ohio Judicial System," 5, http://www.sconet.state.oh.us/Publications/ OJSbrochure.pdf.

40. American Bar Association, *Fact Sheet on Judicial Selection Methods in the States*, accessed December 2, 2017, https://www.americanbar.org/content/ dam/aba/migrated/leadership/fact_sheet.authcheckdam.pdf.

41. Michael Solimine, Carolyn Chavez, Thomas Pulley, and Lee Sprouse, "Judicial Selection in Ohio: History, Recent Developments, and an Analysis of Reform Proposals," in *Report of the Center for Law and Justice at the University of Cincinnati College of Law*, September 2003, 6.

42. "The 2014 Ohio Judicial Elections Survey," Ray C. Bliss Institute of Applied Politics, University of Akron, accessed December 12, 2017, http:// ohiojudicialreform.org/wp-content/uploads/2017/11/BlissSurvey.pdf.

43. "'Name Game' Rules Again in Ohio Supreme Court Races: Editorial," *Cleveland Plain Dealer*, November 7, 2012, http://www.cleveland.com/ opinion/index.ssf/2012/11/name_game_rules_again_in_ohio.html.

44. Maureen O'Connor, "The Ohio Modern Courts Amendment: 45 Years of Progress," *Albany Law Review* 76, no. 4 (2013): 1968.

45. William T. Milligan and James E. Pohlman, "The 1968 Modern Courts Amendment to the Ohio Constitution," *Ohio State Law Journal* 29 (1968): 817.

46. Solimine et al., 10.

47. Quinnipiac Poll, December 12, 2012, http://www.quinnipiac.edu/ institutes-and-centers/polling-institute/ohio/release-detail?ReleaseID=1823.

48. Donald J. Ratcliffe, *The Politics of Long Division: The Birth of the Second Party System in Ohio, 1818–1828* (Columbus: Ohio State University Press, 2000).

49. Libertarian Party in Ohio v. Blackwell, 462 F.3rd 579 (6th Cir. 2006).

50. John Husted, Ohio Secretary of State, "2013 Ohio Candidate Requirement Guide." The secretary of state's office was contacted on March 7, 2013, to further discuss this requirement.

51. Ohio Revised Code 3517.03.

52. John H. Fenton, *Midwest Politics* (New York: Holt Rinehart and Winston, 1966), 114.

53. Ibid., 133.

54. "A Study of Early Voting in Ohio Elections," Ray C. Bliss Institute of Applied Politics, University of Akron, accessed November 11, 2014, http://www.uaakron.edu/bliss/research/archives/2010/EarlyVotingReport.Pdf.

55. Lima v. State, 122 Ohio St. 3rd 155,009-Ohio-2598.

56. Cleveland-Marshall College of Law Library, "Forms of Government," Ohio Local Government Law Resource Guide, accessed October 21, 2014, http://guides.law.csuohio.edu/content.php?pid=412696&sid=3371630.

57. League of Women Voters of Ohio, *Know Your Ohio Government,* 7th ed. (Columbus: Author, 1993).

58. "Ohio's Local Government Funds," accessed November 18, 2017, http://www.olc.org/pdf/OHLocalGovernmentsCCAO.pdf.

59. Office of Budget and Management, http://www.obm.ohio.gov/Budget/stabilizationfund/, accessed December 12, 2017.